Millionaire mission 2024:

Through a simple, step-by-step method, this book teaches smart financial decisions, transforms finances, and helps achieve wealth goals.

Roy R. Joseph

Millionaire's mission

All rights reserved. No part of this publication may be reproduced, distributed, or transmitted in any form or by any means, including photocopying, recording, or other electronic or mechanical methods, without the prior written permission of the publisher, except in the case of brief quotations embodied in critical reviews and certain other noncommercial uses permitted by copyright law.

Copyright © Roy R. Joseph ,2024.

Millionaire's mission

Table of contents

Introduction: What is financial freedom?
- Changing Your Perspective for Financial Achievement

Chapter one
- Why It's Vital to Know Your Net Worth

Chapter Two
- A Cash Flow budget

Chapter Three
- Knowing the Fundamentals of Debt
  - The Psychology of Debt: Its Effects on Emotion and Mind
  - Life After Bankruptcy: Reestablishing Equitable Finances

Chapter Four
- 10 high-demand, high-paying talents

- Unlock Your Earning Potential: 10 Ways to Increase Your Income

Chapter Five
- A crucial manual for creating an emergency fund
- An emergency fund: what is it?

Chapter six
- Investing for the Future: How to Make Your Money Work for You
- What does investing entail?

Chapter Seven
- Why is wealth protection vital?
- Examining the Fundamental Stages of Wealth Protection
- Financial Freedom: What Is It?

Introduction

What is financial freedom?

To be financially free means not needing regular employment and having enough savings, assets, and income to live the life you choose. It's about taking charge of your financial situation and decisions.

A universe of opportunities arises when one is financially free.
Realistic methods for achieving financial independence.
For many, achieving financial independence is a goal. It entails accruing sufficient money, investments, and liquid assets to enable you to live the life you want and achieve your objectives free from the constraints of regular work. When we are financially free, our money works for us instead of against us.

How may one achieve financial independence?

In order to achieve financial independence, you need to pay off your consumer debt, accumulate a safety net of savings, and generate enough passive income from investing in or running your own company to cover your living expenses both now and in the future.

Why is financial independence important?

You may live your life as you see fit when you are financially independent. This is why it is really valuable:

Decreased Anxiety and Stress: For many individuals, financial concerns are a big cause of stress. This pressure is lessened by financial independence, enabling you to concentrate on the things that really count in life.

Greater Freedom and Time: Having financial independence gives you more time. You don't have to accept a job you detest just to make ends meet. You may travel, engage in hobbies, see more of your loved ones, or even volunteer for organizations that align with your values.

Increased Security and Mindfulness: Having money gives you a safety net. Unexpected occurrences such as job loss or health crises become less frightening. You have enough money to withstand these storms and continue living the way you want to.

Increased Control Over Your Life: Having enough money gives you the ability to make decisions that are consistent with your morals. You don't have to worry about financial consequences if you decide to work part-time, launch your own company, or engage in creative activities.

Enhanced General Well-Being: A life that is more meaningful is correlated with financial independence. Having more time for your interests, less worry, and the freedom to achieve your goals are all factors that contribute to happiness and wellbeing.

Financial independence is not about becoming very wealthy. In the end, it's about having the flexibility to live the life you choose, striking a balance between your income and spending, and having the means to meet your needs and goals.

We struggle to meet our most important financial goals due to mounting debt, unexpected expenses, excessive consumer spending, and other issues. Everyone has to deal with these issues, but you may set yourself on the best route to financial health by adopting the following habits:

Set aside money for all of your necessities; follow through on this plan; pay off your credit cards in full to minimize your debt; and keep an eye on your score.

Hire a financial advisor, begin saving, stay up-to-date on tax regulations, establish automatic payments via your employer's retirement plan, and establish an emergency fund.

Be as economical as possible, live within your means, and don't be afraid to ask for or negotiate better deals.

Maintaining your personal items is less expensive than replacing them, so take care of them; more importantly, however, take care of yourself and stay well.

Sufficient Income or Plenty of Assets
When you are financially free, it implies you don't need to work or devote any additional time or energy to earning money in order to cover your living needs and many of your life's ambitions. These might be one or both of the following resources:.

independent earnings
You may be financially independent if you own your own company, get government assistance, or have other sources of consistent income that don't require you to work. Social Security payments are paid each month if you are eligible. Regardless of the amount of time you invest, you may be paid if you have grown your firm to the point where you are able to step back from day-to-day operations. Rent is paid to property owners once a month, while property management often oversees upkeep and bears the risk of renting to a tenant who fails to make one or more payments.

If you make enough money on your own to cover your needs and desires, you are financially free.

Plenty of assets
Generally speaking, investments in stocks, cash in bank accounts, and valuable property are assets that promote financial independence. You must first invest in such assets—typically substantial sums of money spread over an extended length of time—in order to employ them in the process of achieving financial independence. For instance, the majority of financial advisors would advise you that maintaining a consistent 401(k) contribution schedule is essential to your long-term financial security and stability. Many individuals may find this to be the case if they begin investing early enough (in their 20s, 30s, or even 40s). But individuals who put off investing until they are fifty years of age or older will not have enough time to benefit from compound interest's power. When accounting for inflation, their contributions typically do not even double.

Building financial independence with assets may pose a challenge. Consider it a delicate balancing act. In order to have enough money to pay your bills while using this strategy to cover your living expenses and goals, you must sell an asset. If you are unable to sell an asset (real estate, for example) quickly enough to get the money prior to the due date of your debt, complications may ensue. These individuals might be referred to as "cash-poor millionaires" because, while their assets may be worth over $1 million, they are unable to access them quickly enough to put them to use.

When you run out of assets to liquidate before you pass away, it might be a much greater issue. In essence, you won't have any money left over to pay your payments if you deplete all of your assets too quickly.

The majority of financially independent families combine the two strategies. They may have their own source of income, such as social security, a business, or investments in dividend-paying stocks, but they also likely have enough assets in the stock and real estate markets to give them financial security, knowing they have plenty to fall back on in case things get tight.

life objectives
Make a note of the total amount of money (income and assets) required to support your desired lifestyle. Indicate the year in which you want to achieve your goals, as well as whether or not you will need to make payments for them. Your chances of achieving your goals increase with their specificity. Next, work your way back to your current age and set frequent financial milestones. These might be specific monetary savings or newly acquired assets.

Spending Plan
Creating and following a monthly family spending plan is a crucial way to ensure that all expenses are paid on time and that investments and the development of independent income

are proceeding as planned. Creating a regular budget helps you stay on top of your financial goals and strengthens your resolve to resist the urge to overspend. Charge cards and consumer loans with high interest rates pose risks to your efforts to accumulate money. For more advice, you may go over the five crucial budgeting guidelines.

Pay your bills and obligations.
Compared to credit cards and retail store cards, student loans, mortgages, and other comparable loans often have interest rates much lower, posing less of a risk to your financial situation. You might accumulate hundreds of dollars' worth of high-interest debt with credit cards. Being deeply in debt for a long time is the exact opposite of being independent. After all, having debt implies duty and even bondage, which go directly against the notion of financial independence.

Conserve
Prioritize self-payment. That's what financial gurus often advise. Enroll in the retirement plan offered by your work and take advantage of any matching contributions to the fullest. Having an emergency fund (or an automated transfer from your bank account) that you may use for unforeseen expenses is also a great idea, and it can be deposited automatically by your company. Additionally, for an individual retirement account, think about setting up an automatic contribution to a brokerage.

Nevertheless, bear in mind that the recommended amount to save is hotly contested, and under some conditions, the appropriateness of such a fund is even called into doubt.

Invest
Hands down, investing is the most reliable and effective approach to increasing your money. Right now is the perfect

moment to conduct your homework and determine which way to start investing—a 401(k) or an IRA. But get going. That is the most crucial step.

Keep an eye on your credit.
Any interest rate pertaining to credit cards, store cards, auto, truck, or house loans or refinances is influenced by an individual's credit record. It also affects other items, such as life insurance and auto insurance prices. The logical conclusion is that an individual who practices risky financial behavior may also drive recklessly and consume excessively. In fact, those with lower credit scores tend to be more likely to be involved in accidents and file greater claims with their insurance companies than are people with better credit scores. This is not to say that someone with terrible credit is a bad driver, any more than it is to say that a 23-year-old man who is single is not a bad driver. He is young, unmarried, and male; thus, his monthly premiums will be higher. Poor credit is one of the various risk pools that insurance companies take into account when calculating your monthly rate.

Bargain
Many Americans are reluctant to haggle over goods and services because they think it makes them seem cheap. Many foreigners would advise Americans to overcome this cultural barrier. You may be able to save hundreds of dollars per year. Smaller retailers, in particular, are usually amenable to haggling. Good discounts may be obtained by making frequent or large purchases.

Acquire the knowledge that is necessary.
Keep up with market developments and financial news, and don't be afraid to modify your financial investment portfolio as necessary. Knowledge is the strongest line of defense against those who prey on naïve customers in order to make

fast money. To avoid going overboard while using your credit card, be sure you are aware of your credit limit. It is your duty to be informed about such information.

Observe your belongings.
Everything from cars and lawnmowers to shoes and clothes survives longer when you take proper care of your house and belongings. What if you didn't need to purchase shoes and clothes as often as you do? You may spend less money by keeping your automobile longer. Maintenance is the key to saving money.

Live below your means.
It's not as hard as it would appear to adopt a frugal lifestyle by adopting the mentality of getting the most out of life while using less. Many affluent people lead frugal lives in order to obtain their money. Being frugal does not imply choosing a minimalist or dumpster-diving lifestyle or engaging in excessive hoarding. Being frugal means making wise purchases of valuables and taking good care of them.

Seek professional guidance.
Getting professional financial guidance to educate yourself and help you make wise decisions can help you avoid troubles, even if you haven't started building money yet. Numerous trustworthy professionals are ready to assist you for free or at a small cost; these specialists range from authorized financial counselors to nonprofit credit counseling organizations to your local county extension specialist.

Stay healthy.
Some employers only allow a certain number of sick days, so when those days are gone, it's a significant loss of revenue. Illnesses and weight issues drive up insurance costs, and poor health might force an early retirement with reduced benefits.

While taking care of your health won't cure all of your financial problems, it will help you form useful habits that will put you on the path to financial independence.

How Can I Tell Whether I've Reached Financial Independence?

When you can live comfortably without relying on regular work or employment and have sufficient assets or income streams to meet your basic needs and your desired level of discretionary expenditure, you will have reached financial independence. This implies that you are free to work or not work, travel, follow your hobbies and passions, and live your life as you see fit.

You should make a detailed budget that accounts for all of your costs, such as housing, food, utilities, transportation, insurance, and discretionary spending, in order to assess whether you've reached financial independence. After that, you should contrast your total income—which includes money from investments, rentals, and any part-time jobs—with your out-of-pocket spending. In the event that your earnings surpass your outgoings, you can be headed toward financial independence.

It's critical to remember that achieving financial independence is a journey, not a destination, and that achieving your goals may take some time and effort. However, you may attain financial independence and lead the life you've always desired with careful planning, disciplined saving and investment, and a willingness to accept short-term sacrifices.

Changing Your Perspective for Financial Achievement

Financial hardship or excessive debt may cause one to develop a negative and damaging financial thinking process. A person may not even be aware of how this style of thinking affects their money until it has been ingrained in them. If you are always afraid of money, you could jeopardize your chances of earning more money or paying off debt. You need to change your perspective because if you ignore your money entirely, you'll just end up getting further into debt.

Here are some pointers to get you started on developing a good money mentality.

Please pardon your previous financial errors.
No one is flawless. It's likely that throughout the years, you have made a number of poor financial judgments. Maybe you went on too many shopping sprees or overpaid for rent because you fell in love with a gorgeous home, and now your credit cards are completely depleted. All of your previous decisions have already been made. It's possible that past errors are still having an impact on you, but you don't have to constantly criticize yourself for them. Not everyone is taught how to handle money effectively, since it might be difficult. Many individuals learn their lessons by making mistakes. The two most crucial things to concentrate on are self-forgiveness and learning from your errors.

When it comes to the bad choices you've made in the past, you should also attempt to reframe your thoughts. If you are in debt, reflect back on your social gatherings, travel experiences, and educational expenses. You made memories and found joy in your debt. Don't romanticize it, but keep in mind that it has a function. It's neither a hostile place nor an abyss from which you can never return. When you needed it, it was there for you, and now you can work toward paying it off so you can go on with an even better life.

Recognize your thoughts and feelings about money.
Even though you may believe you know how you think about money, a closer examination may reveal some surprising information. Try this: Take a minute to jot down your feelings and thoughts after every purchase or financial decision you make throughout the day. What's going through your mind right now? What is your emotional state? Be truthful and meticulous. When everything is said and done, review everything with an open mind. You may discover that certain areas of your budget are causing you more worry than you anticipated, or you may discover that a purchase you had anticipated would make you happy really made you feel guilty after a little period of satisfaction. While it's perfectly OK to sometimes treat yourself, you should also consider the true impact of your spending patterns on your emotional, mental, and physical well-being.

Understand that it's a losing game to compare yourself to others.
One of the riskiest things you can do in life is to compare yourself to other people; the same goes for money. To begin with, comparisons are seldom precise. There is a warped lens. You are the most knowledgeable person about yourself, but if you compare yourself to a celebrity, an Instagram user, or a fictitious character, you are essentially comparing yourself to someone with whom you are unfamiliar. Facebook is fake. People just show you what they want you to do. They only share the best parts of their financial and personal journeys on

social media. For example, you may come across an Instagram user who shares pictures of their gorgeous house, fashionable clothing, and lavish trips, but you have no idea how much debt they have on their credit cards. You have no idea whether they owe their parents thousands of dollars or are two months behind on their vehicle payments. They won't tell you about that portion of their adventure, so you'll never know. You can see why it is misleading and risky to compare your complete narrative with only a highlight reel of theirs, however, since you are continuously confronted with the darker side of your own.

You're in a comparable situation, even if you're comparing yourself to friends or relatives. You can never really comprehend someone else's financial status or the considerations that go into difficult choices since you can never know as much about them as you do about yourself. Another drawback is that you risk being frustrated if you compare yourself to others and discover that you are losing. Rather than concentrating on the good, you're concentrating on the bad. Your objectives begin to seem unachievable. You pay more attention to your shortcomings than to your progress. These kinds of thoughts have the potential to hinder you and ultimately lead to poorer financial choices.

Strive to develop positive habits.
Don't avoid talking about your money. Instead, make time each week to review your spending patterns, budget, and bills. Emphasize the areas that need development, and give yourself a pat on the back for any accomplishments. Ignoring a problem won't make it go away. Instead, ignore your worries and take on the issues head-on.

Establish reasonable objectives for yourself, and treat yourself modestly when you achieve them. Since neither your success nor your money got out of control overnight, it's critical to establish a number of little objectives and recognize each accomplishment.

Make a budget that makes you happy.
A budget usually causes an individual anxiety. Many see a budget as limiting and restrictive, yet this need not be the case. A flexible budget may help you recognize your limits and keep within your spending limits while still giving you permission to sometimes reward yourself. Generally speaking, you should allocate half of your monthly income to bills and requirements. You should set aside twenty percent of your salary for savings or debt repayment. Thirty percent is yours to do as you please. It may be time to take a closer look at your monthly expenses and see which ones you can reduce or eliminate if you discover that you are unable to stick to this schedule.

Remember to be grateful.
Embrace your current situation and express gratitude for whatever you have, even if it may not be as much as you would want. Give thanks for your vehicle that gets you around, your job that pays your bills, your fridge full of food, your roof over your head, and so on. Money shouldn't rule over you or your ideas. There is always time to increase your income and improve your life, but it won't be enough until you learn to be thankful for what you already have. Rather, you should try to manage the way you think about money so that you can start to better regulate how much you spend. Start with these pointers, and see how your attitudes and ideas about money begin to positively impact your life.

Chapter one

Why It's Vital to Know Your Net Worth

Your net worth is the difference between your liabilities and assets. To put it simply, your net worth is the sum of your assets and liabilities. You have a positive net worth if your assets are greater than your obligations. In contrast, you have a negative net worth if your obligations exceed your assets.

An instantaneous picture of your current financial status is given by your net worth. The total of all the money you have made and spent up to this point will be shown if you compute your net worth today. While this number is useful, analyzing your net worth over time gives you a more insightful picture of your finances. For example, it may serve as a wake-up call if you are entirely off course or a "job-well-done" affirmation if you are doing well.

Your net worth, when computed on a regular basis, may be thought of as a kind of financial report card that helps you assess your present financial situation and determine what steps you need to take to get to your desired financial position.

Salary
Everything you possess that has worth and can be exchanged

for cash is considered an asset. Examples include retirement savings, investments, bank and brokerage accounts, real estate, and personal belongings like jewelry, cars, and collectibles—not to mention cash itself. Sometimes intangibles like your personal network are also regarded as assets. Your debts, including credit card debt, mortgages, medical expenses, and school loans, are represented by your liabilities, on the other hand. Your net worth is the difference between the total value of your assets and liabilities.

Putting a precise valuation on each of your assets is a difficult part of figuring out your net worth. To prevent inflating your net worth, it's crucial to use cautious estimations when assigning values to specific assets (i.e., having an inaccurate perspective of your wealth). For instance, your house is most likely your most valued asset and might have a big influence on your financial status. You may compute a realistic net worth by accurately valuing your house, either by consulting with a skilled real estate agent or by comparing it to other properties in your neighborhood that have previously sold.

Notably, however, there is disagreement over whether or not personal homes should be included as assets when determining net worth. Because these values may be turned into cash in the case of a sale, some financial experts think that your home's equity and market value should be regarded as assets.

However, according to some experts, even if the homeowner did receive money from the sale of the house, they would need to use it to purchase or rent another residence. This basically indicates that the expense of the new dwelling, which is the new responsibility, is incurred with the funds obtained. Of course, a portion of the value of the previous house may be deemed an asset if it is worth more than the new one.

When assigning financial worth, it's advisable to err on the side of caution since it's easy to exaggerate the value of your possessions.

Worth Significant
Your net worth has a wealth of information. If the number is negative, you owe more than you possess. If the balance is positive, you have more assets than liabilities. Your positive net worth will be $150,000 ($200,000 - $100,000 = $150,000) if, for instance, your assets are $250,000 and your liabilities are $100,000. On the other hand, if your obligations total $250,000 and your assets are $100,000, your net worth will be negative ($100,000 - $250,000 = -$150,000). A negative net worth just indicates that you now have more responsibilities than assets, not that you are a careless or irresponsible person.

The same is true for the stock market; your net worth will change. However, much like in the stock market, the general trend is what matters. As you get older, your net worth should ideally increase as you pay off debt, increase the equity in your house, accumulate other assets, and so on. When you start drawing from your assets and savings for retirement income, your net worth will inevitably decrease.

Because every person's financial circumstances and aspirations are different, it is difficult to determine a universally applicable "ideal" net worth. Rather, you'll need to figure out what your desired net worth is and where you want to be, both now and down the road. Some individuals believe that the following calculation helps them determine a "target" net worth if they don't know where to start:

NetWorth target: [Your Age - 25]*[15*Gross Annual Income]
A 50-year-old, for instance, would strive for a net worth of $375,000 ([50 - 25 = 25] x [$75,000 ÷ 5 = $15,000]), given their gross yearly income of $75,000.
This does not imply that the net worth of every 50-year-old

should be equal. You can use the formula as a starting point. Depending on your objectives and lifestyle, your optimal net worth may be much greater or less than the amount suggested by the guideline.

Why It Matters What Your Net Worth Is
You are forced to face the truth about your financial situation when you look at your net worth statements and see the patterns in black and white. You can find out where you are now and how to get to where you want to be by reviewing your net worth statements on a regular basis.

If you are not on track, this could serve as a wake-up call, and if you are moving in the right direction (i.e., decreasing debt while building assets), it could serve as motivation. Getting back on course might include the following:

Spend Caution
Understanding your net worth is critical because it may reveal areas in which you overspend. You are not required to purchase anything just because you can afford it. Before making a purchase, decide if it's a necessity or a desire to avoid racking up unnecessary debt. Your necessities should account for the bulk of your expenditures in order to cut down on wasteful spending and debt. Remember that you may mistakenly justify a desire for a need. While a $500 pair of shoes might meet a need for footwear, you could be better off spending less and still be making progress toward your financial goals with a less costly pair.

Reduce Debt
Taking a close look at your assets and obligations will assist you in creating a debt repayment strategy. For example, you may be paying off credit card debt at 12% interest while receiving 1% interest in a money market account. In the long run, you could discover that it makes sense to use the money

to pay off the credit card debt. When in doubt, do the math and consider the implications of losing access to that money (which you may need for emergencies) to determine if it makes financial sense to pay off a particular loan.

Conserve and make investments.
You may be inspired to save and invest money by your net worth data. You may be motivated to keep going if your net worth statement indicates that you are on track to reach your financial objectives. On the other hand, if your net worth shows that you still have room for improvement—for instance, if over time your assets have decreased and your obligations have increased—it may serve as the impetus you need to start saving and investing more aggressively.

Recognizing Your Revenue and Outlays
Gaining an idea of your income and spending is one of the first steps towards making a budget. Knowing exactly how much money you bring in each month and where it is going is crucial. This will assist you in deciding how best to spend your money and pinpoint areas where you may make savings. In this section, we'll look at some advice on how to understand your income and spending and apply that data to make an effective budget.

Keep a record of your earnings and outlays.
Tracking your income and spending is the first step towards comprehending them. This entails keeping a log of every penny you earn and spend each month. This may be done by handwriting notes in a notebook or by utilizing an app or spreadsheet for budgeting. Make sure to mention all of your income sources, including side gigs, government assistance,

and your pay. List all of your monthly expenditures, including rent, utilities, and food, as well as any sporadic costs, such as auto maintenance or medical bills.

Determine the fixed and variable costs you incur.
Sorting your spending into fixed and variable categories is crucial after you have a list of them. Rent and auto payments are examples of fixed costs that are the same each month. Food and entertainment expenses are subject to change. Knowing the distinction between these two categories of costs can assist you in deciding where, if at all possible, to reduce your expenditure.

Determine your net income.
The money that remains after all of your costs are subtracted from your revenue is known as your net income. This is the amount of money you can save or use for non-essential purchases. To calculate your net income, subtract all of your expenses from your total revenue. You'll need to make some changes to your budget if your spending exceeds your income.

Think about your financial objectives.
It is essential to take your financial objectives into account while drafting a budget. Which goals are you aiming to achieve: debt repayment, retirement savings, or a down payment on a home? Allocating your assets more wisely may be achieved by having clear financial objectives in mind. For instance, you may need to reduce your discretionary spending and put more money into your savings account if your objective is to save for a down payment on a home.

Consider your purchasing patterns.
Lastly, it's critical to assess your spending patterns. Examine your expenses to find places where you can save. Reducing your use of takeout or canceling unused subscription services

might be enough to achieve this. Finding places where you can cut down on your expenses can allow you to have more money for your financial objectives.

Comprehending your earnings and outlays is an essential step in building an effective budget. You can determine how to manage your money and reach your financial goals by keeping track of your income and expenditures, separating fixed and variable costs, figuring out your net income, thinking about your financial objectives, and assessing your spending patterns.

Chapter Two

A Cash Flow budget

A cash flow budget is a helpful tool for organizing how money will be used in the company

An estimate of all anticipated cash inflows and outflows for a certain time period is called a cash flow budget. Estimates may be generated on a monthly, biweekly, or quarterly basis, including both farm-related expenses and non-farm revenue. Cash flow budgeting, on the other hand, disregards profitability and net income in favor of solely looking at money movement.

A cash flow budget is an effective management tool because it:

- compels you to consider your yearly goals.
- evaluates your farming strategies, such as whether you'll make enough money to cover all of your expenses.
- It estimates the amount of operational credit you will need and the time frame for loan repayment.

- gives you a benchmark to measure your real cash flows against.
- helps you explain to your lender your agricultural ambitions and credit requirements.

The majority of individuals need a method to track their monthly spending. A budget may provide you with a greater sense of financial control and facilitate the process of setting aside money for your objectives. The secret is to choose a financial tracking system that you are comfortable with. The procedures listed below will assist you in making a budget.

First, determine your net income.
Your net income is the cornerstone of a successful budget. That is your take-home pay, which is your entire income less any taxes deducted, as well as any employer-sponsored benefits like health insurance and retirement plans. If you focus on your total pay rather than your net income, you may overspend because you will believe that you have more money available than you really do. To help you handle erratic revenue, keep thorough records of your contracts and payments, whether you are a freelancer, gig worker, contractor, or self-employed.

Step 2: Monitor your expenses.
Determining where your money is going is the next step after determining how much of it you are bringing in. You may find out what you are spending the most money on and where you might be able to save the most by keeping track of and organizing your costs.

Make a list of your fixed costs first. These are consistent monthly expenses, such as utilities, rent or mortgage, and auto payments. Next, make a list of your variable costs, which include things like food, gasoline, and entertainment that might vary from month to month. Here are some areas where you may be able to save some money. Since credit card and bank statements often include or categorize your monthly expenses, they are an excellent place to start.

Using a pen and paper, an app on your phone, or online budgeting spreadsheets or templates, keep track of your daily expenditures.

Step 3: Make sensible objectives.
List your short- and long-term financial objectives before you begin going over the data you've recorded. Short-term objectives, such as creating an emergency fund or paying off credit card debt, should be completed within a year to three years. It may take decades to accomplish long-term objectives like investing in your child's college tuition or retirement. Though they don't have to be rigid, knowing what your objectives are can help you stay within your spending limit. For instance, if you know you're saving for a trip, it could be simpler to reduce your spending.

Step 4: Create a strategy.
The difference between what you really spend and what you wish to spend is where it all comes together. Make use of the constant and variable expenditures you gathered to estimate your future spending. Next, contrast it with your priorities and net income. Think about establishing precise, attainable spending limits for every cost category.

To further refine your spending, you might separate your expenditures into necessities and wants. For example, fuel is considered a requirement if you travel to work every day. On the other hand, a monthly music subscription can be considered a wish. When you're trying to figure out how to get money to go toward your financial objectives, this distinction becomes crucial.

Determine your monthly income, choose a technique for creating a budget, and track your development.

Try using the 50/30/20 rule as a basic foundation for budgeting.

Set aside up to 50% of your income for necessities, such as minimum debt payments.

Give them a 30% share of your salary.

Set aside 20% of your salary for savings and higher-than-minimum debt payments.

With frequent check-ins, you can keep tabs and oversee your spending.

Step 5: Modify your expenditures to adhere to your budget.
You can now make any necessary changes to your income and expenditures to ensure that you don't overspend and have money left over to work toward your goals. First, consider making cuts in the direction of your "wants." Is it possible to forego movie night in favor of a home movie? Examine your monthly payment expenditure more closely if you have already made adjustments to your spending based on demands. If a "need" is examined closely, it can merely be "hard to part with."

If the figures don't add up after that, consider modifying your fixed costs. For example, might you save more money if you shopped around for a better deal on homeowners' or vehicle insurance? These selections have significant trade-offs, so carefully consider your alternatives.

Recall that little savings may add up to significant sums of money. One little change at a time might surprise you with how much additional cash you end up with.

Step 6: Consistently review your budget.
Once your budget is established, it's critical to regularly assess both it and your expenditures to make sure you are remaining within your means. There aren't many fixed components to a budget: you may get a raise, your spending might shift, or you might accomplish a goal and wish to put aside money for a new one. Whatever the reason, make it a practice to review your budget on a regular basis by following the guidelines above.

Chapter Three

While debt may be a crippling weight, it doesn't have to control who we are or how we live. With the right information and techniques, we can overcome the difficulties that debt brings by taking back control of our money.

Knowing the Fundamentals of Debt

Understanding the basics of debt is essential before we can manage it well. There are two types of debt: secured debt and unsecured debt. Unsecured debt has no collateral requirements, whereas secured debt is supported by assets like real estate or vehicles.

The significance of interest rates on debt is one important factor. Your eventual repayment amount over time is determined by the interest rates on your credit cards and loans. Understanding how interest rates may affect the amount of debt you accrue is crucial. Since high-interest debt may mount up rapidly, it's critical to pay off these loans first in order to reduce total spending.

It is essential to distinguish between different forms of debt in order to make well-informed borrowing choices. Knowing the hazards associated with each type can assist you in assessing your financial position and selecting the best course of action.

The overall amount of debt you have is greatly impacted by

the interest rates on credit cards and loans. Debt may mount up rapidly due to high interest rates, so it's important to compare rates and terms. You may lower your debt load and save money over time by evaluating many lenders and being aware of the conditions of the loan.

Various Debt Types: Secured and Unsecured
Lenders take less risk when they have collateral, thanks to secured loans. Nevertheless, assets may be forfeited in the event of nonpayment. Conversely, unsecured debt does not need security, yet failure to make payments may result in adverse outcomes, including ruined credit and legal action.

It is essential to distinguish between different forms of debt in order to make well-informed borrowing choices. Knowing the hazards associated with each type can assist you in assessing your financial position and selecting the best course of action.

Interest Rates' Part in the Growth of Debt
The overall amount of debt you have is greatly impacted by the interest rates on credit cards and loans. Debt may mount up rapidly due to high interest rates, so it's important to compare rates and terms. Because various student loan types have varied interest rates, managing student loans may become complicated. For graduates, this means that repayment planning should be smart.

Your credit score is a major factor in deciding interest rates and loan approvals when you borrow money. Lower interest rates and more favorable borrowing arrangements may be obtained by keeping your credit score high. It's critical to comprehend how your credit score is determined and, if needed, take action to raise it.

How Credit Scores Impact Debt and Borrowing

Interest rates and loan approvals are mostly influenced by credit ratings. Lower interest rates and more favorable borrowing arrangements may be obtained by keeping your credit score high.

Your chances of being accepted for better-term loans and credit cards might be increased by learning how credit ratings are determined and taking action to raise your score. This may reduce your total borrowing costs and help you manage your debt more effectively.

Getting Around the Loan Terms and Conditions
A lot of loan agreements include a number of terms and conditions. You may make wiser borrowing choices and steer clear of any unpleasant surprises down the road by being aware of the small print and the related fees.

The terms and conditions of any loan arrangement should be thoroughly read before signing. Pay close attention to specifics like interest rates, repayment plans, and any other costs or expenses. You can choose a loan that fits your budget by being aware of all the conditions and making an informed decision.

The Psychology of Debt: Its Effects on Emotion and Mind

Debt may affect a person's emotions and mental health significantly. Our general well-being might be negatively impacted by the stress and worry that come with having debt. In order to move toward debt management, it is imperative that these effects be acknowledged and addressed.

Stress brought on by debt may have an impact on many areas of our lives, such as relationships, productivity at work, and general happiness. It's important to establish constructive coping strategies and ask for help when required. You may develop a more constructive and long-lasting strategy for handling your financial responsibilities by addressing the psychological and emotional effects of debt.

Case Studies: Actual Examples of Debt Management
Real-world examples may provide priceless insights into effective debt management techniques.

Examining actual debt management cases may provide you with useful advice and methods for efficiently handling your personal debt. These case studies will present several methods of budgeting, financial planning, and debt payback. You may have the confidence to take charge of your financial situation and strive toward being debt-free in the future by learning from the experiences of others.

Techniques for Paying Off Debt
With our newfound knowledge of debt, let's concentrate on practical methods to lessen our financial obligations. The avalanche and snowball approaches are two well-liked ways to pay off debt.

Having a strategy in place is crucial when it comes to debt reduction. By paying off bills in order of greatest to smallest, the snowball technique builds momentum with each obligation paid off. With this method, you may feel motivated and accomplished as your bills start to go away one by one.

You may allocate more money to higher bills by paying off your smaller ones first.

The avalanche technique, on the other hand, gives priority to loans with the highest interest rates. You may be able to save more money over time by concentrating on the debts that are costing you the most interest. This strategy may require more perseverance and self-control because noticeable progress may take longer. Nonetheless, there may be significant cost reductions.

The Debt Repayment Avalanche vs. Snowball Methods
There are benefits and drawbacks to both the avalanche and snowball approaches. By allowing you to experience immediate successes, the snowball technique gives you a psychological lift that may sustain your motivation as you work toward paying off your debt. On the other hand, if you pay off high-interest bills first, the avalanche strategy could end up saving you more money overall.

Which of the two approaches you choose will depend on your financial condition and personal preferences. To choose the right strategy for you, it's critical to evaluate your objectives, top priorities, and available resources.

Methods of Budgeting for Efficient Debt Management
Developing and adhering to a reasonable spending plan is essential for efficient debt management. Intentional spending is made possible by proper budgeting, which also guarantees early debt repayment and gives individuals more control over their personal money.
While making a budget, it's critical to accurately estimate your income and expenditures. Consider all of your revenue sources, such as your salary, bonuses, and any extra sources of money. Make sure to account for all required costs while

creating your budget, including rent or mortgage payments, utilities, food, travel expenditures, and debt repayments.

You may find areas where you can reduce or make modifications after you have a comprehensive view of your revenue and spending. This might include cutting down on frivolous spending, figuring out how to save money on necessities, or looking into methods to get a raise.

Emergency Funds' Function in Debt Prevention
Creating an emergency fund is a crucial part of a sound financial strategy. Having money put aside for unforeseen costs helps lessen the need to take on further debt during difficult times.
Emergency savings serve as a safety net, offering assurance of one's finances and mental stability. An emergency fund ought to be sufficient to cover three to six months' worth of living costs. This guarantees that you won't need to use credit cards or loans to pay for unforeseen expenses like auto repairs, medical problems, or job losses.

You may prevent taking on more debt and concentrate on paying off your present bills by setting up an emergency fund. Prioritizing the establishment of an emergency fund in addition to your debt reduction activities is crucial.

Debt Consolidation Benefits and Drawbacks
Consolidating debts into a single, lower-interest loan is known as debt consolidation. It's important to consider the advantages and disadvantages before making this choice, even if it might make repayment easier and save money on interest.

The ease of managing just one monthly payment is one of the primary benefits of debt consolidation. As a result, keeping track of your progress and maintaining organization may become easier. Furthermore, you could ultimately save money on interest costs if you can use consolidation to get a lower interest rate.

It's crucial to take into account any possible disadvantages of debt consolidation. Your eligibility for a favorable interest rate may be contingent upon your credit score and financial circumstances. Furthermore, many consolidation options, such as home equity loans, may incur costs or require collateral.

Making Sensible Use of Balance Transfer Credit Cards
Credit cards that allow balance transfers provide customers with the opportunity to move high-interest debt to a card with a 0% or reduced interest rate for a limited time. Using balance transfer credit cards sensibly might help you save costs and expedite your debt payback.

Carefully review the terms and conditions of any balance transfer offer before pursuing it. Take note of the interest rate that will be in effect after the promotional period expires, the balance transfer charge, and the introductory period duration.

Make a strategy to pay off the transferred debt within the introductory period to maximize the benefits of a balance transfer. To speed up your debt repayment, you may need to increase your monthly payment or obtain more money. By doing this, you'll be able to fully benefit from the interest savings and get closer to debt freedom.

How to Bargain with Creditors: Strategies and Advice
Sometimes, working out a better repayment plan with creditors might result in more bearable conditions. We'll provide helpful hints and methods for settling disputes with creditors in a way that might lessen debt loads and improve financial freedom.

It's critical to go into negotiations with creditors prepared with a solution in mind as well as a clear awareness of your financial status. Be ready to discuss any difficulties or obstacles that have led to your present financial predicament.
If a new payment plan better suits your present financial situation, think about suggesting a lump-sum payment. Throughout the negotiation process, it's critical to maintain composure and decorum, since doing so might boost the possibility of coming to a mutually advantageous arrangement.

In order to get their money back, creditors could be open to working with you to find a solution that will satisfy both their needs and your ability to pay back your obligations.

Debt's Effect on Personal Finances
The impact of debt on our own budgets is extensive. Making better financial choices and aiming for a debt-free existence may be aided by our understanding of their impacts. Let's examine the several ways debt affects our ability to manage our finances.

Debt has long-term consequences, in addition to affecting your current financial status. A crucial indicator that lenders use to evaluate a borrower's capacity to pay back loans is the debt-to-income ratio. This ratio evaluates the relationship between an individual's income and debt. Knowing this ratio and its importance enables us to carefully manage our debt and make well-informed borrowing choices.

Long-term debt can have detrimental effects on our ability to make ends meet. It may hinder our capacity to invest, save, and accomplish our objectives. For instance, we could find it difficult to save money for emergencies or retirement if a significant amount of our salary is used to pay off debt.

Understanding these impacts may spur us to action and reduce our debt loads.

Additionally, debt is a major factor in our creditworthiness. Our credit scores can be positively impacted by a history of responsible debt management, which can facilitate the acquisition of favorable borrowing terms and other financial opportunities. However, having too much debt or a bad credit history can have a negative impact on our creditworthiness, making it harder for us to get credit and potentially raising the cost of borrowing.

It is imperative to stay out of high-interest debt and payday loan traps. These loans are frequently associated with exorbitant fees and interest rates, making it difficult to break the borrowing cycle. In order to escape this debt trap and preserve financial stability, it is essential to comprehend the risks and look into alternatives.

Financial stress, which is often brought on by debt, may negatively affect our general wellbeing. Both our physical and emotional health may be impacted by the ongoing stress and anxiety brought on by debt. Examining the connection between stress and debt might inspire us to manage our money wisely and strive toward debt reduction. By putting tactics like budgeting into practice, getting expert advice, and looking into debt repayment alternatives, we can reduce financial stress and enhance our quality of life in general.

Debt default may have serious, enduring repercussions. When we don't make the agreed-upon installments on a loan, we are in default. Defaulting may have negative effects on credit ratings, lead to creditor lawsuits, and result in heavier financial obligations. Understanding the possible consequences of debt default is critical, as is exploring solutions to avoid this predicament. Proactive measures may lessen the consequences of default and even avoid them, such as speaking with creditors, looking into debt consolidation possibilities, or requesting aid from credit counseling organizations.

Navigating Debt Relief and Bankruptcy
For people with severe debt, seeking debt relief or contemplating bankruptcy may be important. While these solutions should be carefully explored, they may give people a new start on their journey to financial recovery. Let's investigate these alternatives in greater depth.

Debt may be a terrible burden to shoulder, influencing every part of one's life. It may generate stress, disrupt relationships, and impair future financial aspirations. That's why it's vital to understand the numerous options available for debt relief and bankruptcy.

Exploring Debt Relief Programs and Their Legitimacy
Debt reduction programs may give people support in managing their obligations. These programs provide a variety of services, including debt consolidation, negotiating with creditors, and setting affordable repayment arrangements. However, it's necessary to be careful and verify that the programs picked are trustworthy and connected to their unique requirements.

When considering debt relief options, it's vital to study and check their credibility. Regrettably, there are a lot of con artists and dishonest businesses that take advantage of helpless people looking for debt relief. Before committing to any debt relief program, it's critical to check for certification and glowing testimonials from reliable sources.

The Procedure and Consequences of Bankruptcy Filing

Bankruptcy filing is a big choice that should only be undertaken after giving it serious thought and speaking with experts. When they are unable to repay their obligations, individuals or corporations may seek relief from them via the legal procedure of bankruptcy. Before starting this path toward financial relief, it is crucial to comprehend the procedure and its repercussions.

The consequences of bankruptcy include both short- and long-term. It has drawbacks, including a detrimental effect on credit ratings and the possible loss of assets, even if it offers instant respite from creditor harassment and collection operations. Nonetheless, filing for bankruptcy may also provide people with a new start and the opportunity to reconstruct their financial lives.

Life After Bankruptcy: Reestablishing Equitable Finances

After declaring bankruptcy, the process of becoming financially better starts. Having a strategy in place is crucial to restoring stability and financial health. This includes making a budget, setting up an emergency fund, and cultivating thrifty spending habits.

Reestablishing creditworthiness is a crucial step in the process of emerging from bankruptcy. Even though a bankruptcy may appear on credit records for a number of years, credit prospects are not always lost. People may gradually improve their credit ratings by adopting prudent financial practices, such as paying their bills on time and using their credit sparingly.

The Legal Dimensions of Debt Reduction
In order to settle debts, one must bargain with creditors to pay a smaller sum. For those who wish to stay out of bankruptcy but are unable to pay back their obligations in full, this alternative may be intriguing. Before choosing this course of action, it is critical to understand the legal ramifications and probable implications of debt settlement.

Debt settlement may have both advantages and disadvantages. On the one hand, it may provide people with an opportunity to reduce their debt burden and avoid bankruptcy. However, it may have a negative impact on credit ratings and tax consequences. In order to make an educated choice and completely comprehend the legal ramifications, it is crucial to speak with an experienced debt settlement attorney.

When and How Credit Counseling Services Can Help
Credit counseling services may provide guidance and assistance in properly managing debt. These programs include debt management strategies, budgeting help, and financial education. To guarantee the finest results, it's crucial to understand when and how to contact credit counseling organizations.

Credit counseling may be helpful for those who need expert direction and are having trouble managing their debt. These services may assist people in making a sensible budget, settling disputes with creditors, and formulating a repayment strategy. But it's crucial to choose a trustworthy credit counseling service, and you should be wary of any additional fees or expenses.

Recognizing How Bankruptcy Affects Credit Scores
Although filing for bankruptcy significantly lowers credit ratings, it does not result in a loss of creditworthiness. It's critical to comprehend how bankruptcy affects credit scores over time and how to regain creditworthiness after filing for bankruptcy.

The length of time a bankruptcy remains on credit reports varies based on the kind of bankruptcy filed. It could be difficult to get fresh credit or loans during this period. Nonetheless, people may raise their credit scores gradually by rebuilding credit and adopting good financial practices.

After filing for bankruptcy, credit may be restored through regular payments, minimal credit use, and responsible credit use. Additionally, it's critical to routinely check credit reports for accuracy and take quick corrective action when necessary. These measures may help people gradually restore their creditworthiness and financial stability.

Avoiding further debt
In order to achieve long-term financial success, controlling and paying off current debt is just as important as avoiding debt in the future. A debt-free future may be achieved by putting sound financial practices into place and building a solid financial foundation.

Developing sound financial practices to avoid debt
Creating sound financial practices is essential to avoiding debt in the future. We'll look at doable methods for building a strong financial foundation, such as keeping track of spending and setting aside money for emergencies.

Financial Literacy's Significance in Debt Prevention
The foundation for making wise financial decisions is financial literacy. Gaining a better grasp of personal finance enables us to make wise decisions, stay out of debt, and create a stable financial future.

Establishing and following a reasonable budget
Creating a realistic budget is one effective strategy for guaranteeing prudent spending and avoiding unnecessary debt. We'll talk about how to make a budget that works and fits our priorities and financial objectives.

Emergency Preparedness: Getting Ready for Unexpected Costs
Unexpected costs have the potential to make us debt-ridden. Creating a solid emergency plan enables us to be ready for unforeseen events in life and prevents financial losses from becoming chronic liabilities.

The Function of Insurance in Debt Protection
Insurance acts as a crucial barrier against unforeseen costs and possible debt. We can avoid the financial consequences of unanticipated catastrophes by being aware of the many forms of insurance available and determining the coverage that is necessary.

Prudent Expenditure: Mindful Consumption as a Debt Dissuader
Making conscious decisions about our purchases and ensuring that they support our financial objectives and beliefs is the essence of mindful spending. By adopting a responsible consumer attitude, we can avoid unnecessary debt and build a more contented and secure financial future.

In conclusion

When it comes to handling and conquering debt, information really is power. We may take charge of our financial health by being aware of the many kinds of debt, practical methods for reducing it, and how debt affects our individual budgets. We may create a future free of debt by investigating choices like debt relief and bankruptcy and concentrating on avoiding future debt via sound financial practices. Remember that there is always a way to become financially free, regardless of how crushing debt may feel.

Chapter Four

10 high-demand,high-paying talents

Keeping up with the newest trends and innovations is crucial to staying ahead of the competition in today's fast-paced employment environment. Learning new, in-demand skills is essential to keeping a competitive edge and raising income potential. Certain abilities may become obsolete as new jobs and industries develop, necessitating adaptation and the acquisition of new ones.

In 2024, professionals should master 10 high-demand, high-paying talents to remain ahead of the curve and manage the ever-changing employment environment. These abilities have been shown to be essential for both pay potential and professional advancement, and they may aid people in being hired and promoted.

1. Information analysis
Proficiency in data analysis is necessary across several contexts and vocations, including responsibilities in leadership and management. Gaining expertise in this area might help one pursue a career as a data analyst. This position requires the ability to visualize, extract, model, clean, and understand complex data so that decision-makers can use it. This facilitates the development of informed strategies by organizations. In today's data-driven environment, data

analysis is an essential component of decision-making processes.

2. Organizing the project
Project management is a highly sought-after skill set in many different businesses around the world. Up to 2032, there will be a 6% increase in the demand for project managers, who will need to possess outstanding organizational, methodical, risk-management, relationship-building, team-building, cooperation, and communication abilities.

3. UI/UX Design
The user experience and user interface design of mobile and online applications are crucial for facilitating seamless consumer interactions in today's tech-driven culture. UX/UI design is an essential skill set that ensures customer satisfaction for the customers and users of public and private sector organizations, educational institutions, and enterprises in general. As of October 2023, Statista estimates that there will be almost 5.3 billion internet users worldwide. In order to make sure that goods satisfy customer demands, it entails doing user research, designing aesthetically pleasing and simple interfaces, and testing them.

4. Online advertising
Proficiency in digital marketing is vital to attracting prospective clients and fostering their interaction with a company's offerings. These abilities call for originality as well as a commitment to client interaction. You possess digital marketing talents if you are passionate about content development, influencer marketing, graphic design, social

media interaction, or video editing. It is advised that you attend digital marketing courses, particularly ones that are niche-specific, to hone these abilities. By doing this, you may gain the knowledge necessary to develop successful digital marketing plans that will enable you to connect with your target market.

5. Artificial intelligence, or AI
Artificial intelligence (AI) is a formidable technology with vast potential that has been incorporated into almost every sector and kind of organization. AI has the potential to boost global economic production by $2.6 trillion to $4.6 trillion, according to a McKinsey & Company analysis.

To upskill in AI, it's not always necessary to pursue years of education to become an AI scientist or machine learning engineer. In order to accomplish business and career objectives, it is crucial to understand contemporary applications of AI within one's particular work environment. This will improve job quality and production, cut down on wasted time, and employ AI in situations that reveal industry insights.

Some of the most sought-after AI competencies are:

Natural language processing (NLP)
Robotic Learning
Automation
Computer Vision
In-depth Education

AI is a very flexible and in-demand skill set that can be used in many different industries, including healthcare, finance, manufacturing, and more.

Unlock Your Earning Potential: 10 Ways to Increase Your Income

I'll go over some tried-and-true methods for boosting your earnings and reaching financial freedom.
Prior to getting started, however, it's critical to realize that earning more money isn't the only option to boost your revenue. It also involves cultivating the attitude and abilities required for financial success. In light of this, let's examine some essential actions you can take right now to start earning more money.

Determine your interests and strong points.
Determining your abilities and hobbies is the first step towards boosting your earnings. What skills come easily to you? What activities do you find enjoyable? You have a better chance of succeeding in your career and landing a job that you love and find important if you concentrate on your hobbies and areas of strength.
If you're naturally good at solving problems, you may want to look into a job in customer service or consulting. A profession in marketing or advertising could be something you should think about if you're creative. And if you have a strong desire to serve others, you can think about pursuing a career in teaching or social work.

Expand your knowledge and abilities.

After determining your talents and interests, building your knowledge and abilities in those areas is the next step. This might include going to school, getting a degree, or just learning from experience and independent research.

To become a good salesman, for instance, you can think about enrolling in a course on psychology or sales strategies. Consider getting a marketing degree or enrolling in a social media marketing school if you want to work in the field of marketing. Additionally, you can think about enrolling in an entrepreneurship or business strategy course if you want to become a successful entrepreneur.

Make connections and cultivate ties.

Developing connections and networking is essential to raising your revenue. Making connections with people in your field may help you advance your career, find out about new possibilities, and get guidance and assistance.

Numerous methods exist for networking and establishing connections, such as going to business gatherings, becoming a member of professional organizations, and making connections on LinkedIn. By offering superior customer service and serving as a valued resource, you may also cultivate connections with clients, customers, and coworkers.

Discover new sources of revenue.

Seeking methods to diversify your revenue streams is crucial in addition to your main source of income. This may include launching a side business, buying stocks or real estate, or simply renting out a room on Airbnb.

You may lower your financial risk and raise your earning potential overall by identifying new sources of income. For instance, having a profitable side business selling handcrafted goods online can provide you with a backup income stream to support you through any financial difficulties.

Make a wage or increase negotiations.
You may be able to increase your income by asking for a raise or better pay if you currently have a job that you like. Though it may seem daunting, it's crucial to keep in mind that you should be compensated fairly for your services.

Make a list of the going prices for your job in your industry, so you know what to ask for. Next, have a friend or family member help you rehearse your pitch. Be prepared to support your request with evidence of your achievements, talents, and service to the firm.

When negotiating, keep in mind to act with decency and professionalism and attempt to emphasize the value you contribute to the organization rather than merely asking for more money. You may want to think about volunteering to take on extra duties or projects as part of your negotiations.

Boost your output and effectiveness.
Another strategy for increasing revenue is to work harder and more efficiently. You can take on more work or customers, finish your present task more quickly and efficiently, or do more in less time if you can do more in less time.

There are several strategies to improve your efficiency and productivity, such as utilizing time management software and to-do lists, making a timetable and following it, and clearly defining your objectives and goals. To help you remain focused and prevent burnout, you may also try methods like the Pomodoro Technique, which includes working in short spurts followed by brief pauses.

Take on more duties and difficulties.
Accepting new tasks and responsibilities at work may increase your productivity and efficiency while earning more money. This might be taking on extra volunteer work, going for leadership roles, or even launching your own company.

You can show your company how valuable and capable you

are by accepting new tasks and responsibilities, which will increase your chances of getting a raise or promotion. Additionally, you may gain new experiences and abilities that will increase your marketability in the employment market.

Promote your freelance abilities and offerings.
You may become a freelancer and charge more for your abilities and services if you don't want to work for someone else. Setting your own prices and working on your terms might be facilitated by doing this.
Finding customers who are prepared to pay for your talents and services is essential to being a successful freelancer. This might include networking with possible customers, developing a website or social media presence to highlight your work, and successfully promoting your services.

Make an investment in your own learning and growth.
Lastly, investing in your own learning and growth is one of the finest methods to raise your income. This might include going to school, getting a degree, or just reading books and listening to professionals in the field.
You may increase your earning potential and be more prepared to take on new chances if you are always learning and developing your abilities. Additionally, you'll be more marketable on the employment front and more likely to draw in higher-paying customers or employers.

As you can see, there are several approaches you may use to boost your earnings and succeed financially. There are many ways to start increasing your income right now, including figuring out what your strengths and passions are, developing your knowledge and skills, networking and forming relationships, finding new sources of income, negotiating for a raise, taking on more challenges and responsibilities, offering your skills and services as a freelancer, or making an investment in your own education and development.

Recall that earning more money isn't the only way to boost your income. It also involves cultivating the attitude and abilities required for financial success. You may take charge of your financial destiny and begin experiencing true financial success by using the techniques described in this section.

Chapter Five

A crucial manual for creating an emergency fund

All of us have encountered unforeseen financial crises, such as a car accident, an unanticipated medical cost, a broken appliance, a reduction in income, or even a broken mobile phone. No matter how big or small, these unforeseen costs often seem to come at the worst moments.

One of the most important things you can do to protect yourself is to start saving money by designating a savings or emergency fund. You can recover faster and resume progress toward your broader savings goals by setting aside money, even a modest amount, for these unforeseen costs.

An emergency fund: what is it?

A cash reserve put up expressly for unforeseen costs or financial problems is known as an emergency fund. Medical expenses, house repairs, auto repairs, and income loss are a few typical examples.

Generally speaking, you may utilize emergency savings for any unexpected expenditure or payment that isn't included in your regular monthly spending and expenses.

Why is it necessary for me?
If you don't have savings, even a little financial setback might cause you problems down the road, and if it results in debt, that damage could not go away.

According to research, those who have a hard time getting over a financial setback tend to have fewer reserves to help them weather another disaster. They could rely on loans or credit cards, which may result in debt that is often more difficult to repay. To meet these expenses, they could also take money out of other investments, such as retirement accounts.

How much of it do I need?
Depending on your circumstances, you may need to establish a larger emergency savings account. Consider the most common types of unforeseen expenditures you have encountered in the past, as well as their associated costs. This might assist you in determining your desired amount to put away.
Setting money aside might be challenging if you don't get paid the same amount every week or month or if you live paycheck to paycheck. However, even a small sum may provide some monetary stability.

Find the savings strategy—or strategies—that are most effective for you by reading on.

How should I construct it?
There are several ways to begin saving money. These tactics address a variety of circumstances, such as having little capacity to save or having inconsistent income. You may be able to employ all of these tactics, but the simplest methods to get started are to manage your cash flow or set aside some of your tax return if you don't have much to save.

Technique: Make saving a habit.
Being able to save regularly makes it simpler to accumulate funds of any amount. It is one of the quickest methods in this manner. If you don't already save on a regular basis, here are some essential guidelines for developing and maintaining a savings habit:

Establish a goal: Having a clear objective for your savings can keep you motivated. Setting up an emergency fund might be a doable objective that keeps you on course, particularly in the beginning. Depending on how much and how frequently you are able to save, you may use our savings planning calculator to determine how long it will take you to attain your goal.

Establish a mechanism for regular contributions: There are many methods to save money, and one of the simplest is often to set up automatic repeating payments, as you'll see below. Another option is to set aside a certain amount of money every day, week, or pay period. Set a goal for a certain amount, and your savings will increase much more quickly if you can sometimes afford to do more.

Track your progress frequently. Establish a routine for

checking your funds. Finding a mechanism to track your progress may provide satisfaction and motivation to keep going, whether it's by writing down a running tally of your donations or receiving an automated alert about your account balance.

Celebrate your victories. If you're remaining true to your savings routine, don't pass up the chance to acknowledge your achievements. Choose a few self-care techniques, and after you've accomplished your first objective, decide on your next one.

Who can benefit from this? Anyone, but those who have a steady income are especially encouraged. You may make it a habit to contribute a portion of your paycheck, or any income you get on a regular basis, to an emergency savings account.

Method: Control your money flow.
The time when your money comes in (from your revenue) and leaves (from your costs and spending) is what makes up your cash flow. Inaccurate timing may result in you running out of money at the end of the week or month, but if you monitor it often, you'll start to realize where you can make adjustments to your savings and expenditures.

You might be able to negotiate with your creditors (landlords, utility providers, credit card companies, etc.) to change the dates on which your payments are due, or you could utilize the weeks when you have more money to transfer a little amount into savings.

Who can benefit from this? Everyone. Whether you're living paycheck to paycheck or you tend to spend more than your budget permits, this is an essential first step in managing your money.

Strategy: Utilize one-time chances to save money.
Additionally, there can be periods of the year when you get a large windfall. A tax refund is often one of the biggest checks that people in the United States get each year. You could get a monetary present at other times of the year, such as on a birthday or holiday.
Even though it would be easy to spend it all, keeping some or all of the money might enable you to swiftly accumulate emergency funds.

Who can benefit from this? Everyone, but those with inconsistent income in particular. Always think about placing all or part of a substantial check you receive in the mail for a tax return or any other reason.

Technique: Set up automatic savings.
Setting up an automated savings account is one of the easiest ways to start saving consistently and see your funds grow over time. Setting up recurring transfers via your bank or credit union to transfer money automatically from your checking account to your savings account. You will be consistently contributing to your savings after you have it set up, although you get to choose how much and how frequently.

But it's a good idea to keep an eye on your balances to avoid paying overdraft penalties in the event that your checking account is depleted of funds at the time of the automated transaction. To stay alert, consider adding calendar reminders or automated alerts to remind you to check your balance.

Who can benefit from this? Anyone, but those who have a steady income are especially encouraged. Again, you are in charge of deciding how much and how often to move money between accounts, but you should always ensure that you are receiving money. If your circumstances or income change, you can always modify it.

Plan: Put money aside via labor.
You can also set up automatic savings for your job. Apart from the employer-based retirement payments, you may be able to divide your salary between your savings and checking accounts. If you get your paycheck via direct deposit, ask your company if splitting it between two accounts is feasible. This is a simple approach to saving money aside without giving it much thought if you're tempted to spend your salary right away.

Those with steady incomes are the ones for whom this is beneficial. Once again, if your company sends you a check on a regular basis, pay yourself first by setting aside some of it automatically for savings.

What location should I store it in?
It depends on your circumstances and where you place your emergency money. This money should be kept in a location where it is secure, easily accessible, and unlikely to be spent on non-emergencies.
You may choose the option that best suits your needs from the following alternatives for where to place your emergency savings:

Bank or credit union account: It may make sense to have a specific account where you can retain and manage these monies if you have an account with one of these institutions, which are often seen to be among the safest locations to deposit your money.

A prepaid card allows you to put money in it. You can only spend what is on your card, and it is not affiliated with any bank or credit union.

Cash: Keeping emergency cash on hand, either at home or with a reliable family member or friend, is an additional choice. Remember that money may be lost, stolen, or destroyed.

Sprouting plants from coin and bill stacks

When am I supposed to use it?
Decide for yourself what expenses are emergencies. Even if every unforeseen cost isn't an immediate crisis, try to maintain consistency. You could need it to cover a medical expense that wasn't covered by insurance, even if it's not an ER visit.

You may be able to stay out of debt by keeping a reserve of cash for unforeseen expenses rather than depending on loans or other credit options. Your one-time emergency spend might end up being much more than your initial payment if you use a credit card or take out a loan to cover these costs because of interest and other penalties.

But if you need it, don't be scared to use it. Simply put, if you deplete your emergency funds, attempt to replenish them. If you practice saving over time, it will become easier.

Chapter six

Investing for the Future: How to Make Your Money Work for You

What does investing entail?

In general, investing is the act of allocating resources, usually capital (i.e., money), with the expectation of generating an income, profit, or gain; it is the process of putting money to work for a period of time in some sort of project or undertaking in order to generate positive returns (i.e., profits that exceed the amount of the initial investment).

Investing may take various forms (directly or indirectly). For example, one might use capital to launch a company or buy assets like real estate with the intention of renting them out and/or selling them at a profit in the future.

Investing and saving are not the same thing. Investing involves putting money to work, which implies an implicit risk that the associated project or projects could fail and result in a loss of capital. Speculation, on the other hand, does not involve putting money to work per se; rather, it involves betting on short-term price fluctuations.

Learning how to invest
Investing is the process of growing money over time. Its fundamental tenet is the expectation of a positive return in the form of income or a statistically significant price increase. There is a vast array of assets in which one might invest and generate a return.

The two terms "risk" and "return" are synonymous in the investing world; lower risk typically translates into lower expected returns, while higher returns typically translate into higher risk. At the low-risk end of the spectrum are basic investments like Certificates of Deposit (CDs); bonds or fixed-income instruments are higher on the risk scale, whereas stocks or equities are considered riskier. Commodities and derivatives are generally the most risky investments.

Within an asset class, risk and return expectations might differ significantly. For instance, a micro-cap listed on a smaller market would have a considerably different risk-return profile than a blue-chip listed on the New York Stock Exchange.

The returns that an asset generates vary depending on its type. For example, bonds typically pay interest every quarter, whereas many equities pay quarterly dividends. Additionally, various sources of income are taxed differently in many countries.

The total return from an investment can therefore be thought of as the sum of income and capital appreciation. Standard & Poor's estimates that since 1926, dividends have contributed nearly a third of the total equity return for the S&P 500, while

capital gains have contributed two-thirds. Price appreciation is an important component of return in addition to regular income, such as a dividend or interest.
For this reason, capital gains are a crucial component of investment.

Economists see investing and saving as two sides of the same coin. This is because, when you save money by putting it in a bank, the bank lends it to people or businesses that want to borrow it for legitimate purposes, so your savings are frequently invested in by someone else.

Investment Types
These days, investment is mostly linked to financial instruments that enable people or companies to raise and provide cash to enterprises, who then use the funds for expansion or revenue-generating endeavors.

Although there are many other kinds of investments, the following are the most popular ones:

Stocks
Purchasing stock entitles a buyer to a portion of the company's earnings; stockholders, often referred to as owners, may take part in the development and success of the business via dividend payments made from time to time from the company's profits and stock price increase.

Bonds
Bonds are the financial obligations of businesses, governments, and municipalities. Purchasing a bond entails assuming ownership of a portion of the debt of an organization and is entitled to interest payments on a regular basis as well as the repayment of the bond's face value upon maturity.

Money
Investment managers oversee funds, which are pooled instruments that allow investors to make investments in stocks, bonds, preferred shares, commodities, and so on. Mutual funds and exchange-traded funds, or ETFs, are the two most popular types of funds; mutual funds are valued at the end of the trading day and do not trade on an exchange, while ETFs trade on stock exchanges and are valued continuously during the trading day. Both mutual funds and ETFs can be actively managed by fund managers, or they can passively track indices like the S&P 500 or the Dow Jones Industrial Average.

Trusts for Investments
A trust is another form of pooled investment. One of the most well-known types of trusts in this category are Real Estate Investment Trusts (REITs), which invest in residential or commercial real estate and distribute money to investors on a regular basis based on the rental income these properties generate. Since REITs are listed on stock exchanges, they provide investors with immediate liquidity.

Alternative financial positions
Hedge funds and private equity are two examples of alternative investments. Hedge funds are named after their ability to use leverage to offset investment bets; private equity allows businesses to raise capital without going public. Traditionally, only wealthy individuals who satisfied certain income and net worth requirements were granted access to hedge funds and private equity. However, in recent years, alternative investments have been made available to retail investors through fund formats.

Alternative Derivatives and Options

Derivatives are financial instruments that derive their value from another instrument, such as an index or stock. One common type of derivative is an options contract, which gives the buyer the right, but not the obligation, to purchase or sell a security at a fixed price within a predetermined window of time. Since derivatives typically involve leverage, they are considered high-risk, high-reward investments.

Goods and Services
Commodities can be traded through commodity futures, which are agreements to buy or sell a specific quantity of a commodity at a specified price on a particular future date, or through exchange-traded funds (ETFs). Commodities can be used for speculative or risk-hedging purposes. Commodities include metals, oil, grain, and animal products, as well as financial instruments and currencies.

Comparing Approaches to Investing
Let's contrast two of the most popular investment approaches:

While there are advantages and disadvantages to both strategies, in practice, few fund managers outperform their benchmarks sufficiently to warrant the higher costs of active management. Active investing aims to "beat the index" by actively managing the investment portfolio. Passive investing, on the other hand, advocates a passive approach, such as purchasing an index fund, in tacit recognition of the fact that it is difficult to beat the market consistently.
Growth versus value: Value investors seek out companies with significantly lower PEs and higher dividend yields than growth companies, as the latter may be out of favor with investors for an extended period of time. Growth investors, on the other hand, prefer to invest in high-growth companies, which typically have higher valuation ratios, such as price-earnings (P/E).

How to make investments

Self-Doing Investing
If you are a Do-It-Yourself (DIY) investor or would rather have your money managed by a professional, the answer to "how to invest" is simple: many investors who would rather manage their own money have accounts at discount or online brokerages because of their low commissions and the ease with which trades can be executed on their platforms.

Investing on your own, also known as self-directed investing, involves a certain level of knowledge, expertise, time, and emotional restraint. If any of these qualities don't sound like you, it could be wiser to hire an advisor to handle your money.

Expertly handled investing
Professional money managers charge their clients a percentage of assets under management (AUM). Although professional money management is more expensive than managing one's own money, these investors are willing to pay for the convenience of having an expert handle their research, trading, and investment decision-making. Typically, these investors have wealth managers looking after their investments.

Investors are advised to verify the licensing and registration status of their investment professionals with the SEC's Office of Investor Education and Advocacy.

Investments with a Robotic Advisor
Some investors choose to follow the recommendations of automated financial advisors (robo advisors). Robo advisors,

which are driven by artificial intelligence and algorithms, gather information about investors and their risk tolerance in order to make appropriate recommendations. Because they operate largely without human intervention, they provide an affordable alternative to human investment advisors. As technology advances, robo advisors can now assist clients with retirement planning, trust management, and other retirement accounts, including 401(k)s.

A Synopsis of Investing's Past
Although the idea of investing dates back thousands of years, the modern form of investing emerged in the 17th and 18th centuries as the first public markets were developed to link investors with investment opportunities: the Amsterdam Stock Exchange was founded in 1602, and the New York Stock Exchange (NYSE) in 1792.

Investments in the Industrial Revolution
The greater prosperity that followed the Industrial Revolutions of 1760–1840 and 1860–1914 allowed people to save money that could be invested, which in turn led to the development of an advanced banking system. The majority of the well-known banks that now dominate the investment world, such as Goldman Sachs and J.P. Morgan, got their start in the 1800s.

Investing in the 20th Century
New ideas in asset pricing, portfolio theory, and risk management emerged during the 20th century, and many new investment vehicles—such as hedge funds, private equity, venture capital, REITs, and exchange-traded funds (ETFs)—were introduced in the second half of the century.

The public gained access to online research and trading tools in the 1990s due to the Internet's fast expansion, completing the democratization of investment that had started over a century earlier.

Modern-Day Investing
The 21st century was ushered in and perhaps set in motion by the burst of the dot.com bubble, which produced a new generation of millionaires through investments in technology-driven and online business stocks. The collapse of Enron, with its full display of fraud that bankrupted the company and its accounting firm, Arthur Andersen, as well as many of its investors, took center stage in 2001.

The Great Recession of 2007–2009, which caused a massive number of failed investments in mortgage-backed securities to collapse, crippled economies globally, bankrupted well-known banks and investment firms, increased the number of foreclosures, and widened the wealth gap, is one of the most significant events of the twenty-first century, if not all of human history.

The 21st century saw a proliferation of low-cost online investment firms and free-trading applications, like Robinhood, which allowed novices and nontraditional investors to explore the world of investing.

Speculation vs. Investing
Three criteria determine whether purchasing a security counts as speculation or investing:

The level of risk assumed: Compared to speculation, investing often entails a lesser level of risk.
The investment's holding term: speculation usually entails considerably shorter holding periods, but investing usually includes a longer holding period, often expressed in years.
Source of returns: In speculative investing, price appreciation

is often the primary source of returns; nevertheless, dividends or distributions may account for a significant portion of investment returns.

Given that price volatility is a common way to measure risk, buying a conservative blue-chip and expecting to hold it for a few years would be considered investing; buying a cryptocurrency with the intention of flipping it for a quick profit in a few days, on the other hand, would be clearly considered speculating.

An Illustration of an Investment Return
Since XYZ does not pay any dividends, let's say you bought 100 shares of its stock for $310 and sold it for $460.20 precisely a year later. Your anticipated total return, excluding fees, would be ($460.20 minus $310) x 100% = 48.5%.

If, on the other hand, XYZ had paid out $5 in dividends per share throughout the time you were holding the stock, your estimated total return would have been 50.11% (capital gains: 48.5% + dividends: ($500/$31,000) x 100% = 1.61%).

How Can I Invest My First Money?
Investing can be done in one of two ways: either you do it yourself and choose the investments based on your investing style, or you hire an investment professional, like an advisor or broker. First, you should decide what kind of investments you want to make and how much risk you are willing to take; if you are risk averse, then stocks and options might not be the best option. Next, you should create a strategy that outlines your goals and preferences for how much, how often, and what to invest in. Finally, before you allocate your resources, make sure the target investment is in line with your strategy and has the potential to yield the desired results. Remember, you don't need a lot of money to start, and you can adjust it as your needs change.

What Kinds of Investments Are There?
Investment options abound; stocks, bonds, real estate, and ETFs/mutual funds are among the most popular. You should also think about real estate, CDs, annuities, cryptocurrencies, commodities, collectibles, and precious metals.

How Can My Money Grow With Investing?
Investing doesn't have to be done by affluent people. You can make small investments, like buying cheap stocks, putting small sums of money into an interest-bearing savings account, or saving until you reach a target amount to invest. If your employer has a retirement plan, like a 401(k), set aside small amounts of your income until you can increase your investment. If your employer matches, you might find that your investment has doubled.

You can start investing with as little as $1,000 and make significant returns. For example, if you invested $1,000 in Amazon's initial public offering (IPO) in 1997, you would now have millions of dollars. This is partly because of multiple stock splits, but it doesn't change the fact that the returns were enormous. Savings accounts are accessible through most financial institutions and don't usually require a large initial investment. The best savings accounts are those with the most features and competitive rates.

Investing $1,000 in real estate doesn't have to mean buying an income-producing property; you can put your money into a real estate investment trust (REIT), which is a business that invests in and manages real estate to generate income and profits. You can use $1,000 to buy REIT stocks, mutual funds, or exchange-traded funds.

Are investing and gambling the same thing?

No, there are significant differences between gambling and investing. Investing involves putting your money to work in activities or projects that are expected to yield a positive return over time; investing has a positive expected return. On the other hand, gambling involves placing bets on the results of games or events; your money is not being put to work at all and frequently has a negative expected return. While an investment may lose money, it will do so because the project involved fails to deliver; on the other hand, the outcome of gambling is solely random.

The final word

Investing is putting money, assets, cryptocurrency, or other forms of exchange into something in order to generate income or make a profit. Depending on your goals and risk tolerance, you can choose between a variety of investments, with lower returns for assuming less risk and higher returns for assuming more risk. Examples of investment types include stocks, bonds, real estate, precious metals, and more.

Different investment instruments have varying degrees of risk and return, including stocks, bonds, mutual funds, and real estate.

Via technology, investors may now get automated investing solutions via robo advisors, or they can choose to work with a certified and registered investment adviser. Alternatively, they can invest autonomously without the assistance of a professional.

A huge number of vehicles have cut their minimum investment requirements, making participation more accessible. Nevertheless, the amount of consideration, or money, required to invest varies heavily depending on the kind of investment and the investor's financial status, objectives, and ambitions.

a list of tasks to complete:

Establish financial objectives: Knowing your objectives will help you choose the right kind of investments for you. Are you saving for a down payment on a home? Are you planning for retirement? Are you building an emergency fund? These are just a few examples of the financial goals you should have before you start investing.

Recognize the various investment options: There are numerous investment options, such as stocks, bonds, real estate, and mutual funds. Each of these options has a unique set of risks and potential returns, so it's critical to conduct due diligence and weigh the advantages and disadvantages of each.

Spread your investments across various asset classes and industries to minimize risk. This is one of the fundamental principles of investing. By diversifying your portfolio, you can lessen the impact of a single underperforming investment on your entire portfolio.

Create a risk management strategy: Investing in the stock market always has some risk, so it's important to have a plan in place to manage that risk. Some strategies to consider include diversifying your portfolio, buying a combination of growth and value companies, and limiting your losses using stop-loss orders.

Think about collaborating with a financial advisor. Investing can be difficult and time-consuming; a financial advisor can guide you through the process and help you make wise decisions about your investments. They can also help you develop a customized investment plan and offer advice on how to reach your financial objectives.

Be patient and adhere to your plan. Investing is a long-term strategy, and it's crucial to keep in mind that stock market fluctuations might occur. Even when the market is down, you should remain committed to your plan.

Assess and rebalance your portfolio frequently. It's important to periodically assess your portfolio and make any required modifications to guarantee that your investments continue to be in line with your objectives and risk tolerance.

You can make your money work for you and reach your financial goals by learning the fundamentals of investing, creating a plan, and consulting with a financial advisor. Investing can be a great way to build wealth over time, but it's important to be smart and strategic about your investments.

.

Chapter Seven

Everyone wants to live comfortably and provide for their loved ones, so we all want to protect and grow our wealth. But creating and maintaining wealth is not without its difficulties and risks; this is where insurance and estate planning come into play. In this extensive guide, we will explore the value of wealth protection, the function of insurance, and the significance of estate planning in safeguarding your financial future.

Let's discuss how to attain long-term financial stability by protecting your money and making wise judgments.

Why is wealth protection vital?

Building money takes commitment, diligence, and thoughtful preparation. After you have a sizable asset accumulation, it is critical to safeguard your wealth against unanticipated events and possible hazards. Money protection is important for a number of reasons:

1) Emergency preparedness: Unexpected events like illnesses, accidents, or natural disasters can have a significant negative influence on your financial situation. If you have the right wealth protection strategies in place, you can make sure that you and your loved ones will have access to money in hard times.

2) Preserving your legacy: Wealth protection encompasses more than simply safeguarding your current assets; it also aims to protect and preserve your legacy for future generations. Through prudent wealth management and protection, you may transfer your money to your heirs and facilitate a seamless asset transfer.

3) Minimizing financial risks: One of the most important aspects of asset preservation is managing and diversifying your investments. By doing so, you can reduce the impact of market volatility and possible financial dangers.

I'm sure you've realized by now how important it is to preserve your money, so let's talk about the finest strategies for doing so.

How should your wealth be protected?
Investing, risk management, and careful planning are just a few of the many tactics that make up a complete approach to asset protection. Here are some important approaches to preserving your money:

1) Diversification: One of the cornerstones of wealth protection is diversifying your investments. You can reduce the risk of large losses and attain long-term growth by distributing your portfolio among various asset classes, including stocks, bonds, real estate, and commodities.

2) Risk Management: Identifying possible risks, such as inflation, market volatility, or regulatory changes, enables you to take proactive steps to lessen their influence on your financial stability. Risk assessment and management are critical components of wealth preservation.

3) Asset preservation: Another important part of wealth preservation is insulating your assets from any legal responsibilities. You may do this by using legal structures like limited liability corporations (LLCs) and trusts, which can protect your assets from creditors and litigation.

4) Insurance: Let's examine insurance's function in safeguarding your money in more detail. Insurance is a fundamental component of asset protection and provides financial security in the event of unanticipated circumstances.

Comprehending Insurance for Wealth Protection
Any complete wealth management plan must include wealth protection insurance, which consists of several insurance coverages intended to safeguard your assets and provide you with financial stability. Some popular forms of wealth protection insurance are:

1) Life Insurance: Life insurance guarantees that your loved ones will have financial assistance even in the event that you are no longer able to give it to them by paying out a payment to your beneficiaries upon your death.

2) Health Insurance: Health insurance protects your finances in the case of sickness, accidents, or medical crises by paying for medical costs.

3) Disability Insurance: Disability insurance protects your money by guaranteeing that you will always have a consistent income in the event of a disability that prevents you from working.

4) Long-Term Care Insurance: This insurance shields your assets from being drained by long-term medical bills by paying for nursing homes, assisted living facilities, and in-home care. It also covers the costs associated with prolonged medical treatment.

How Is Your Wealth Protected by Insurance?
Here are some ways that insurance safeguards your wealth: Insurance serves as a safety net, offering peace of mind and financial security.

1) Financial Stability: Whether it's medical bills, legal fees, or property damage, insurance guarantees that you are protected from major financial setbacks. In the event of unanticipated events, insurance provides financial stability by covering expenses that could otherwise deplete your savings.

2) Asset Preservation: Having the appropriate insurance coverage in place can help you avoid selling off valuable assets to cover unforeseen expenses by lowering the need to liquidate them during difficult times.

3) Risk Mitigation: When you pay your premiums on time, you transfer the financial burden of potential losses to the insurance provider, freeing you up to concentrate on accumulating and protecting your wealth.

After discussing the function of insurance in wealth protection, let's delve into the finer points of estate planning and the fundamental phases of wealth protection.

Examining the Fundamental Stages of Wealth Protection

Developing a strong wealth protection strategy requires an understanding of the various stages that comprise the ongoing process of wealth protection. The following are the fundamental stages of wealth protection:

1) Assessment and Evaluation: This phase of wealth protection helps you identify the areas that need immediate attention and create a customized protection plan by evaluating your assets, assessing your current financial situation, and identifying potential risks.

2) Risk Management: Following your financial situation assessment, the next phase is all about reducing possible risks. To do this, you should diversify your investments, put insurance in place, and use legal structures to safeguard your assets.

3) Monitoring and Adjustments: Continual observation of your financial plan and the implementation of appropriate adjustments are essential components of wealth protection. Changes in the economy, your lifestyle, and other external circumstances may call for adjustments to your protection plan.

You can guarantee a stable financial future by navigating these phases and managing your wealth wisely. Let's now discuss estate planning and its importance in wealth management.

Make an impression on your customers by presenting invoices in a distinctive and polished manner.
The best invoicing solution created, especially for business owners, is Invoice Temple.

The role of estate planning in wealth management

Estate planning is an integral part of wealth management that focuses on preserving and distributing your assets. It involves creating a comprehensive plan to transfer your wealth to your chosen beneficiaries smoothly. Here's what you need to know about estate planning:

1) Defining Estate Planning: Estate planning is the process of organizing your affairs to ensure the orderly management and distribution of assets after your death. It involves creating legal documents, such as wills, trusts, and powers of attorney, that outline your wishes and instructions.

2) The Role of Wills and Trusts: Wills and trusts are essential components of estate planning. A will allows you to specify how your assets should be distributed, designate guardians for minor children, and appoint an executor. Trusts, on the other hand, provide more flexibility and control over the distribution of assets while also enabling you to potentially minimize estate taxes.

3) Considering Taxes and Beneficiaries: Estate planning involves taking into account potential tax implications and ensuring that your beneficiaries are protected. Strategies such as gifting, charitable giving, and the establishment of trusts can help reduce the tax burden on your estate and ensure that your loved ones receive maximum benefits.

How is estate planning done?

While estate planning may appear daunting, breaking down the process into simple parts will help assure its effective completion. Here is a step-by-step approach to estate planning:

1) Inventory and Assessment: Start by taking stock of your assets and establishing their worth. This includes real estate, investments, retirement accounts, life insurance policies, and personal things. Assess your obligations and existing debts as well.

2) Designating Beneficiaries: Decide who you want to inherit your assets from and distribute them appropriately. Consider any specific circumstances or constraints you may wish to put on the distribution of assets.

3) Creating a Will: Draft a legally binding will that explains your desires for asset distribution, guardianship of children, and the appointment of an executor. Ensure that your will complies with the legal requirements of the country in which you live.

4) Establishing Trusts: If required, set up trusts to preserve and manage your assets. Trusts may provide greater flexibility, control, and protection for your heirs while possibly decreasing inheritance taxes.

5) Appointing Power of Attorney: Appoint someone you trust to make financial and healthcare choices on your behalf in case of incapacitation. A power of attorney guarantees that your desires are honored, even if you are unable to articulate them yourself.

6) Reviewing and Updating: Regularly evaluate and update your estate plan as your circumstances change. Life events such as marriage, divorce, the birth of children, or obtaining major assets may require adjustments to your plans.

While you may develop a basic estate plan on your own, it is best to obtain professional guidance from an estate planning attorney or a financial adviser. They can guide you through the process, verify that your paperwork is legally sound, and help you make educated choices.

The need for estate planning
Estate planning is not only for the rich; it is vital for anybody who desires to safeguard their assets and guarantee their loved ones are cared for. Here's why estate preparation is crucial:

1) Asset Distribution: Estate planning enables you to decide how your assets will be disbursed after your death. Without a plan in place, your assets may be subject to probate court processes, resulting in delays and perhaps undesired distributions.

2) Minimizing Conflicts: A detailed estate plan decreases the risk of arguments among family members about wealth distribution. By clearly articulating your desires, you may help avoid conflicts and promote family peace.

3) Tax Efficiency: Incorporating tax planning tactics into your estate plan will help decrease estate taxes, leaving more wealth for your heirs. Professional assistance can assist you in optimizing your estate plan for tax efficiency.

4) Charitable Giving: You may make a lasting contribution to organizations and causes that are meaningful to you by creating a charitable trust or by adding charitable bequests to

your estate plan.
You may make sure that your desires are followed, your loved ones are taken care of, and your assets are safeguarded by making estate plans.

A proactive approach is necessary to safeguard your wealth and ensure your financial future. You can confidently navigate the complexities of wealth preservation by taking proactive steps to protect your wealth, such as diversification, risk management, insurance, and estate planning.

I have covered the value of insurance in protecting your assets, the role of wealth protection in wealth management, and the role of estate planning in wealth management in this extensive guide. You can safeguard your wealth, leave a lasting legacy, and secure your financial future by incorporating these strategies into your financial plan.

Assessing your financial status, looking into insurance, and deciding whether or not estate planning is necessary are the first steps you should take. Speaking with experts in these fields will give you the direction and knowledge required to design a customized wealth protection plan that fits your priorities and goals.

As always, strategic preparation and action are the keys to growing and maintaining wealth. Protect your capital now for a better financial future down the road.
In summary

Building a nest egg that will allow you to retire or pursue any career you want—without being driven by the need to earn a certain amount each year—is another important goal for many people. Financial freedom is having enough savings, investments, and cash on hand to afford the lifestyle you want for yourself and your family.

Financial Freedom: What Is It?

Everyone has their own definition of financial independence, but for most individuals, it means having enough cash, assets, and savings to support a certain lifestyle, plus a retirement fund or the ability to pursue any vocation without having to meet a minimum wage requirement.

Too many people, sadly, fall far short of financial freedom. Even in the absence of sporadic financial emergencies, mounting debt from excessive spending is a continual burden that prevents them from achieving their objectives. When a major crisis completely upends plans, like a hurricane, earthquake, or pandemic, more gaps in safety nets are exposed.

Problems arise for almost everyone; however, the following behaviors may help you get back on track:

1. Establish life objectives.
What does it mean to you to be financially free? Everyone wants to be financially free, but that's a pretty generic objective. You need to be more precise about what you want and when you want it. The more detailed your goals are, the more likely you are to achieve them.

Put these three goals down in writing:
- What your way of life demands
- The amount of money you need in your bank account to enable that.
- When is the cutoff age for saving so much money?

Next, carefully record all amounts and deadlines, and place the goal page at the front of your financial binder. Count backwards from your deadline age to your actual age and set up financial mileposts at regular intervals between the two dates.

2. Establish a spending plan each month.
The easiest method to make sure that all of your expenses are paid and your savings are on track is to create and adhere to a monthly family budget. It's also a regular ritual that will help you stay motivated to resist the impulse to indulge.

3. Complete credit card payment
Paying off credit cards and other high-interest consumer loans in full each month is essential. Student loans, mortgages, and other similar loans usually have much lower interest rates; it is not an emergency to pay them off. Nevertheless, making timely payments on these lower-interest loans is still crucial, as it will help you establish good credit.

4. Establish autonomous savings
Your first priority should be taking care of yourself. You should join your employer's retirement plan and take full advantage of any matching contribution benefit—basically, free money—as well as setting up automatic withdrawals into an emergency fund that you can use for unforeseen expenses and contributions to a brokerage account or something similar.

The money for your retirement and emergency funds should

ideally be taken out of your account on the same day that you are paid, keeping it entirely out of your hands.

Remember that the recommended amount for an emergency fund varies depending on your specific situation; additionally, tax-advantaged retirement accounts have restrictions that can make it difficult to access your money in an emergency, so you shouldn't use that account as your only source of emergency funding.

5. Get investing right away.
Though bear markets, or bad stock markets, might make individuals doubt the logic of investing, there has never been a better method to grow money historically. Compound interest alone has the ability to increase money enormously, but it can take a long time to attain substantial growth.

The ultimate aim of financial management is financial independence, which may be very challenging in the face of mounting debt, unexpected expenses, health problems, and overspending, but it is achievable with discipline and careful preparation.

6. Monitor your credit report.
When refinancing your house or purchasing a new automobile, the loan rate you are given depends greatly on your credit score.
It also affects the cost of a number of other necessities, such as life insurance and auto insurance.

A person with hazardous financial habits is assumed to be reckless in other aspects of life as well, such as not taking care of their health or even driving after drinking, which is why credit ratings are so important.
Because of this, it's critical to periodically get a copy of your

credit report to ensure that no inaccurate negative information is tarnishing your reputation. To safeguard your credit, it can also be worthwhile to investigate a reliable credit monitoring service.

7. Bargain for Products and Services
Overcome the fear of appearing cheap when negotiating for goods and services, and you could save thousands of dollars annually. Small businesses are especially amenable to negotiation, so taking advantage of bulk discounts and establishing yourself as a loyal customer can lead to favorable terms.

8. Continue your education on money matters.
Knowledge is also the best defense against scammers who prey on unsophisticated investors in an attempt to make quick money; review pertinent changes in tax law to ensure that all adjustments and deductions are maximized each year; stay up-to-date on financial news and developments in the stock market; and do not hesitate to adjust your investment portfolio accordingly.

9. Take Care of Your Assets
The cost of maintenance is a fraction of the cost of replacement, so it's an investment not to be ignored. Proper property care extends the life of anything from vehicles and lawnmowers to shoes and clothing.
Acquire the ability to distinguish between necessities and wants.

10. Make Do with Less Than You Can
Learning to live frugally is all about adopting a mentality that is centered on making do with less, and it's not as hard as you may think. In fact, many affluent people learned to live below

their means before they became wealthy.

Adopting a minimalist lifestyle isn't difficult; all it requires is learning to discern between the things you really need and the ones you just desire, and then making modest changes that add up to significant improvements in your financial well-being.

11. Consult a financial advisor.
Get a financial counselor to help you continue on the correct track if you've reached a point where you've accumulated a respectable amount of money, either in the form of fixed assets (property or anything that cannot be readily converted to cash) or liquid assets (cash or anything easily converted to cash).

12. Look after your health.
The adage "maintenance is necessary" also applies to your body, and maintaining great physical health has a major beneficial influence on your financial well-being.
Investing in your health is not hard; it only requires regular check-ups with physicians and dentists, as well as heeding medical advice regarding any challenges you may experience. A healthy diet and increased activity may help prevent or treat many medical conditions.

On the other hand, poor health maintenance can have detrimental effects on your financial goals over time. For example, some companies have limited sick days, which means that once paid days are used up, you lose your job. Obesity and other dietary illnesses can cause insurance premiums to skyrocket. Finally, poor health can force you to retire early and live with a smaller monthly income for the rest of your life.

www.ingramcontent.com/pod-product-compliance
Lightning Source LLC
Chambersburg PA
CBHW070204230526
45471CB00002B/806